Hits and Sacrifices

poems by

Bruce W. Niedt

Finishing Line Press
Georgetown, Kentucky

Hits and Sacrifices

Copyright © 2016 by Bruce W. Niedt
ISBN 978-1-944251-74-1 First Edition
All rights reserved under International and Pan-American Copyright Conventions. No part of this book may be reproduced in any manner whatsoever without written permission from the publisher, except in the case of brief quotations embodied in critical articles and reviews.

ACKNOWLEDGMENTS

"New Season", "Groundskeeper", "Randy Johnson Kills a Bird", and "Nine Innings" were previously published in *Spitball*, and "Baseball in Manzanar" was published as Poem of the Month for November 2013 on their website.

"Last Spring" was published in *Chantarelle's Notebook* (June 2015).

"Rolling Rock" is a trademark of Latrobe Brewing Company.
"Campbell's Soup" is a trademark of the Campbell's Soup Company.

Thanks to all the poets and editors whose influence, guidance and support have contributed, in big and small ways, to the existence of this book, including Billy Collins, Jane Hirshfield, Donald Hall, Mike Shannon, Kendall and Christinia Bell, BJ Ward, Tammy Paolino, Susanna Rich, and Robert Lee Brewer.

Editor: Christen Kincaid

Cover Art: Jeremy Niedt

Author Photo: Jeremy Niedt

Cover Design: Elizabeth Maines

Printed in the USA on acid-free paper.
Order online: www.finishinglinepress.com
           also available on amazon.com

Author inquiries and mail orders:
Finishing Line Press
P. O. Box 1626
Georgetown, Kentucky 40324
U. S. A.

Table of Contents

New Season 1

Now Batting 2

Between Starts 3

Groundskeeper 4

Ball Park Vendor 5

Haiku/Senryu 6

Tanka 7

Twenty Games Back: A Haibun 8

Two "Free" Shadormas 9

Polo Grounds, August 16, 1920 10

Magic Mud 11

Baseball in Manzanar 12

Mickey Mantle 1965 13

The Ball that Never Came Down 14

Randy Johnson Kills a Bird 16

Score Sheet 17

Hero 18

Another Long Season 19

Walt's Shadow 20

Last Spring 21

Options 22

Nine Innings 23

November, Post-season 26

This book is in memory of three of my favorite Phillies fans: Linda DeVaull, John J. Ward, and Bill Hinshillwood.

New Season

Two feet of snow melt so slowly,
receding like a hairline, day by day,
and as the weather starts to turn
with calendar pages to March,
we see hints of bare ground,
a reminder of what our world
looked like before winter white.
In this field, signs of last summer
begin to peek between shrinking drifts.
Streams trickle off a small hill
in the middle of the clearing,
and a bald spot grows in the sun.
In a few days, we will see evidence
of perpendicular paths, describing
a square, or rather, a diamond.
The grass beyond will reveal itself,
brown, waiting to green,
and when it wakes it will whisper,
then declare like a mandate,
play ball, play ball,
Play Ball.

Now Batting

You stroll from the on-deck circle
as your walk-on music blares
from the stadium speakers:
"Iron Man" by Black Sabbath.
They've just brought in their closer
to play the averages, lefty to lefty.
He's eyeing you, his pupils laser pointers.
His hand fidgets behind his back, rubbing
the ball intently with his thumb.
You glare back and plant your feet
three feet apart in the batter's box,
your legs two pistons ready to push off,
biceps tightening, hands squeezing
into the pine tar on your bat. You take
a couple of practice swings, imagining
the ball slightly down and away, just where
he likes to throw it for a first-pitch strike.
He peers in at the catcher, gets the signal,
and nods. He sets his feet on the rubber
and sizes you up. You return his steely stare.
He rears back. Here's the pitch.

Between Starts

> *Poets are like baseball pitchers. Both have their moments.*
> *The intervals are the tough things.*
> —Robert Frost

Four days rest is an eternity.
I worry about starting this next poem.
Do I still have my best stuff?
If I do, I can blow readers away
with a fastball-metaphor so clever
that all they can do is watch it
whiz by them and mumble, "Wow."
Other days, I'll struggle to get
anything across the plate.
Confidence is like a pitching arm—
when it's strong, you're unstoppable.
If it stiffens up, you can barely
hold a pen. But I'm not out to win
a Cy Young or a Pulitzer. I'd be happy
just to win more than I lose.

Groundskeeper

I cut the diamond
with the precision of a jeweler.
I mow crisscross patterns in the outfield,
the grass to uniform height.
I make sure all facets of the field
are perfect—the foul lines, the batter's box,
drawn meticulously in chalk paint.
I rake and level infield dirt with the patience
of a Zen gardener. I protect my gem, too,
when it rains, pulling the vast tarp over
with my cohorts, a huge black cloak
against the weather. I want it to look pristine
at game time, so all of you in the stands
can admire its geometric simplicity,
so all eighteen or more of you on the field
can kick it up, dig out divots with your cleats,
slide big commas into the sand,
and rough up the lines at home plate,
while I sit stoically out of the limelight,
waiting to polish it all over again.

Ball Park Vendor

I fulfill your dreams
of tasty ice creams
to eat.

This August day steams
but my freezer deems
it sweet.

Your eight-year-old beams
in spite of his team's
defeat.

Haiku/Senryu

1.
Star-spangled Banner—
while the shortstop sings along
the pitcher chews gum

2.
time called—
a stray cat
steals second base

3.
extra innings—
manager swats at a bee
with a scorecard

4.
spring rain
nourishes the outfield—
no game today

Tanka

pitcher peers home for
fingers flicking between knees—
the catcher's signals

on the postgame subway home
a guy and girl exchange looks

Twenty Games Back: A Haibun

It isn't for lack of trying. Their white-and-red uniforms are smeared with grass stains and dirt from diving and sliding. Their gloves are well-worn, and their bats crack loud as anyone's, when they crack at all.

home team scoreboard
a long line of zeroes
blue moon overhead

Second full moon of August hangs over the stadium, a giant fly ball moving on an imperceptible upward arc into the evening. No one will catch it. Banks of lights throw a harsh glare on the field.

center field flags
flap in humid night breeze
no pennant this year

Two "Free" Shadormas

1. Free Agent

Please note that
I'm on the market.
Offer me
megabucks—
I'll be your team's big asset
till the next contract.

2. Free Pass

I wait for
opportunities.
Some are less
than perfect,
and if I let four go by,
I can talk a walk.

Polo Grounds, August 16, 1920

Before you left for the road trip
from Cleveland to New York,
you and your young wife looked
at the new house being built for you.
She was expecting your first child,
and you told her you would retire soon
to raise your kids and join the family business.
Just a few days later, you lay on the ground,
blood oozing from your ear.
Mays had delivered his submarine pitch,
hurling the muddy, stained baseball
through the twilight from mound to plate.
They say you never saw it,
which is why you didn't move
as the pitch cut in on you.
When Mays heard the crack,
and the ball squibbed back to him,
he thought he'd heard the bat,
not your skull, and he threw to first
for the putout. You managed to stumble
to your feet, then collapsed again,
and they rushed you to the hospital,
where you died hours later.
They all took off their caps for you,
Ray Chapman, as you passed through
this game into the next.

Magic Mud

Ever since poor old Chapman got beaned,
they'd been looking for something
to take the sheen off the ball,
so it wouldn't slip dangerously,
even fatally, from the pitcher's hand.
Then in '38, Lena Blackburn of the A's
found me in his favorite fishing hole
across the Delaware. I was the perfect agent:
smooth enough to buff the white to gray,
yet not harsh enough to scratch the leather.
Lena and his successor sent cans of me
to all the major league teams, and ever since,
every baseball has had my imprint.
I was there for Lou Gehrig's last hit,
and Jackie Robinson's first, Don Larsen's
perfect game, and Hammerin' Hank's
714th homer. I was there for Halladay's
two no-hitters, and Jeter's 3000th hit.
I'm part of the pregame ritual,
giving each ball a mud bath and a rub-down.
I'm a proud South Jersey native,
one without equal, never duplicated,
scooped up from a secret sweet spot
near the river, strained, cured and canned,
and sent to thirty teams who would never
start the game without me.

Baseball in Manzanar

When I was twelve we played sandlot ball
in my little town in California.
After the game, I would go to the docks
and help my father with the catch
on his fishing boat. A year later we were
in the desert, in a government compound
bordered by towers and electrified fences.

My father had everything taken from him,
but he said they could not take our pride.
We still played baseball, with a vengeance—
teams and leagues and uniforms, just as
we would have done back home. One day
I almost hit a homer over the barbed wire fence.
A guard in the tower gave me a thumbs-up.
My father said, *They think we're trying too hard
to be Americans. They don't know I played baseball
as a boy back in Kyoto. It's a Japanese game too.*
I said, *Papa, we are Americans.*

My father died too early, never the same
since he lost his business. I grew up,
went to college, married, had three kids,
and now, six grandkids, the oldest of whom
is a college professor. When I think back,
sometimes I still get angry at my country,
but it's still my country. I still watch baseball,
and I have my favorite players, like Ichiro,
who marches inevitably to the Hall of Fame.

Mickey Mantle 1965
(after "The Dance" by William Carlos Williams)

In John Dominis' photo, "Mickey Mantle 1965",
the great slugger, who has been struggling,
slouches slack-jawed toward the dugout,
another strikeout behind him, and his limp right wrist
has just flung his helmet, which hangs in the air
like a lopsided Frisbee, while the blond hairs
on his right forearm catch the afternoon light,
and maybe bad knees or the bottle have taken their toll,
but there is still something defiant about him,
as Clete Boyer waits on deck with two bats,
and the crowd is silent in the early summer haze,
in John Dominis' photo, "Mickey Mantle 1965".

The Ball That Never Came Down

August 6, 1974: Key West hosts
a game between two minor league teams,
the hometown Conchs and St. Petersburg Cardinals,
on a particularly windy evening.

In the bottom of the first,
Joe Wallis of the Conchs hit a high fly ball that arcs
and drifts toward the glove of John Crider,
the Cardinals right fielder.

Crider can't find the ball,
and ducks defensively, while the other outfielders
rush in to back him up. They can't see it either.
Wallis rounds the bases.

The umpire calls a home run,
but the Cardinals argue. The ball is missing in action.
No one remembers hearing it fall. No one remembers
catching it in the stands.

Key West is a town
of ghost stories that sits on a corner of the Bermuda Triangle,
so everyone has their theories. Gary Templeton,
the future Cardinals great

who played infield in that game,
said half-jokingly, "Maybe a UFO took it." Bruce Sutter,
in the dugout that night, and the Hall of Fame today,
swears that it happened.

Maybe the wind,
clocked at twenty knots that night, blew it out to sea,
right into the infamous Triangle. Maybe a wormhole
opened over the stadium

and the ball is still falling
from the evening sky in some other universe
where an outfielder is wondering where the hell
that high fly came from.

Randy Johnson Kills a Bird
(March 24, 2001)

Pity the unlucky dove that decided
to swoop down between home plate
and the mound, just as Johnson released
a ninety-mile-an-hour fastball.
Halfway between origin and destination
for both bird and ball, one could plot
the intersection of two curves,
one graceful and inverted,
one flattened out by sheer speed,
and at that intersection,
an explosion of feathers.

People laugh at the video today
but I'm sure Johnson was shaken up
when the bewildered ump called "no pitch".
What else was there to do but clean up
the mess and continue the game?
The odds against such a meeting
were astronomical, but the universe
is a cruel and funny thing.
We plot our own parabolas every day
not really knowing what will intersect them—
drunk driver, aneurysm, asteroid.
All we can do is move along
and avoid fastballs when we can,
as we try to complete the arc.

Score Sheet

A guy I know, a baseball fan,
self-proclaimed ladies' man,
has taken the baseball metaphor—
"first base", "second base", et cetera—
one step further, keeping score sheets,
sabermetric pages, filled-in diamonds
of all his conquests.

This one is labeled "Jill":
he got a stand-up double,
but was stranded without another hit.
With Alyssa, he says, he got to third,
then stole home. And Jennifer
he describes as a "grand slam"—
I don't even want to know what *that* means.
He brags about his perfect games,
how he blew them all away with his fast ball,
and his line drives up the middle.
"I'm the free agent of love," he says.

But the other team
has kept box scores on him too.
They've recorded all their sacrifices,
but also tallied up his strikeouts, errors, losses,
his foul balls, and a bat that isn't big enough,
as well as why he never made the playoffs,
and all the times they sent him to the showers.

Hero

Forget those things I said about
the home runs that you've hit,
how you never are an easy out,
that you're muscular and fit.

Forget about the time I said
you're wizard with the glove,
you chase balls like a thoroughbred
with hustle that we love.

Forget the times that I was pleased
you won all those awards,
World Series rings and MVP's
and tricked-out custom Fords.

Forget the glowing things I'd say
to praise you as a true
role model for the kids who'd play
to grow up more like you.

Forget all that, it's all erased;
those drugs, your hangman's rope.
So why, if you're the one disgraced,
do I feel like the dope?

Another Long Season

S. is a slacker, D. is a drag,
W. can't hit his way out of a bag.
P. is a slowpoke, B. is a bum,
G.'s a good shortstop, but boy is he dumb.
C. is a closer who can't save a game,
N. has been called every kind of bad name.
R. is a choker, H. a hot dog,
L. hustles less than a hollowed-out log.
O.'s overpaid, V.'s over-the-hill,
U.'s been suspended for using some pill.
F. is a flake, M. plays for the money,
K. strikes out so much it's not funny.
These guys haven't given me reason to cheer;
all I can say is: Just wait till next year!

Walt's Shadow

> *"I see great things in baseball.
> It's our game, the American game."*
> —*Walt Whitman*

In a pocket of a troubled city,
along a rejuvenated waterfront,
you will find a minor-league field
named after the local industry, Campbell's Soup.
Just a few blocks away is the home
of Camden's most famous resident,
the poet who spent his last years here
revising *Leaves of Grass*.
The local team takes its name
not from the poet, or even the soup,
but a rare species of fish, the river shark.
No one has ever found such a creature
in the nearby Delaware, the river spanned
by a big blue suspension bridge
which looms just past the outfield
and takes us to Philadelphia,
home of the bridge's namesake,
Ben Franklin. Walt has a bridge too,
crossing the river just south of here.
All this is backdrop for the game
in a family-friendly stadium,
where we watch players who hope
for glory days to come, and others
who remember theirs. They play into
the evening, as lengthening shadows
of city buildings, including a certain
humble home on Mickle Avenue,
cross the field. And if you look
hard enough through the twilight,
you may see the silhouette
of a bearded old man in a floppy hat,
cheering from the bleachers.

Last Spring

We looked out, Bill and I, from our balcony
on Tampa Bay. Below us, a tiki bar clattered
with spring-breakers, jet skis growled
and drew arcs in the bright water that reached
from our room to the ball park in Clearwater,
which hugged the horizon. We drove
the long causeway, mere feet above the bay;
had breakfast at Lenny's, teeming with Phillies fans;
then watched the game unfold with the afternoon—
blankets on the lawn beyond the right field fence,
where the sun baked us in mid-March,
and once, a home run ball dropped in to our left.
Later, we drove to the beach.
One more thing off my bucket list, said Bill,
who hadn't told me he was feeling ill again,
as we walked the gentle surf of the Gulf
that seemed to stretch into forever.

Options

Every day on that geometrical field
they are faced with options:
fast or curve, change-up or slider,
bunt or swing away, pinch-hitter
or let the pitcher bat, steal or stay put,
catch that looper on one hop
or try for the diving catch
and a chance to be on the weekly highlights.
But the biggest decision is whether to retire
or to tough it out for another season.
Some guys don't have an option:
another torn ACL, too many shoulder surgeries
may force the issue. But most just get too old
and slow and aching to face another spring.
That's where I am right now,
not on a diamond, but in a square cubicle,
and I'm ready to hang up not a pair of spikes,
but a pen and keyboard, and make way
for some up-and-coming rookie.

Nine Innings
(After Donald Hall)

1.
I will pick up the gauntlet, Donald,
and speak in nines, and talk of baseball,
and a life intertwined with that sport
so much so that to separate them
would be like ripping the red stitching
and letting the cowhide fall off.
You'd see a tightly wrapped core, a mile
of string, a cork center. I don't want
to be peeled away so nakedly.

2.
Like you with your Red Sox, I've suffered
almost fifty years a Phillies fan,
the losses and the cellar-dwelling,
the occasional winning season.
Never a good player, not even
for Little League, I still loved to watch
my home team in gorgeous black-and-white,
as Jim Bunning blew the Mets away,
perfect game, Father's Day '64.

3.
But the other side of '64
is the Big Collapse. Six-and-a-half
games up with a week to play, and they
lose the pennant to the Cardinals.
My thirteen-year-old heart breaks, but not
for the last time. There will be girlfriends,
high school and college, which I survive
with some fair success, while my Phillies
flirt with mediocrity and worse.

4.
Seventy-three: at a stopgap job
in a men's store, I wait on the Phils'
third baseman Cesar Tovar, on the
DL with a sprained thumb. Soon they will
replace him with some kid named Mike Schmidt.
The team begins to build itself up
to a contender, while my life builds
up with marriage, a child, a career.
But they lose three times in the playoffs.

5.
Vindication in 1980!
Their first-ever World Series title!
Schmidty, Lefty, Bull, Charlie Hustle,
Tug, Bowa, Maddox—all my heroes.
We celebrate in a bigger home,
two more boys on the way. I take my
oldest to his first game, but at five
the only thing that impresses him is
the Phillie Phanatic's zany shtick.

6.
Another Series in '83,
but this time we lose. Years of doldrums
follow, when we think that fashion is
big hair, big glasses, big shoulder pads.
I struggle to fight midlife crisis,
easy to catch as a common cold.
Ninety-three: rough bunch in the Series—
Schilling and Kruk, Dykstra and Daulton—
then Joe Carter homers off Williams.

7.
Donald, you still mourn your dear wife Jane,
she who would fall asleep by the fifth.
When my future wife took me to meet
my future father-in-law, she said,
Talk baseball—it will make you fast friends.
Summer evenings, we'd sit on the screened
back porch, Rolling Rock bottles in hand,
swatting intruder mosquitoes, as
gray TV light danced on our faces.

8.
When I was a kid, my grandmother
took me to Connie Mack Stadium.
She worked for Campbell Soup, who would have
company nights at the park. We watched
from the nosebleed seats—Richie Allen,
Johnny Callison, Tony Taylor—
or back at her house, the radio
issued the mellow voice of By Saam.
She was a Phillies fan to the end.

9.
They both would have loved the '08 team,
the second championship. Howard,
Utley, Rollins, Hamels beat the Rays
after two days of rain. Donald, now
it's the top of your ninth, and it's my
seventh-inning stretch—kids grown, good wife
by my side. And I got to see this:
the final out, wild celebration,
Lidge on his knees, bear-hugged by Ruiz.

November, Post-season

Even the best of them packed up last week.
Mine was done by the end of September—
before that, really. Today I sneak in
through an unlocked gate. The only action
I see is from the groundskeepers, fertilizing
and seeding the outfield, getting it ready
to survive the coming winter. No bases
on the diamond, no rubber on the mound.
The press boxes are dark, the stands empty—
blank stares from the seats and backs of chairs.
The lockers are cleaned out, doors half-open
like raided sarcophagi. Everything here echoes.
All the jerseys have been shipped out,
the bats and balls, gloves and catchers' masks.
The players are home with their families;
some of them will play winter ball.
I find an old ticket stub in my pocket—June 6th,
Dollar Hot Dog Night, when we were still
optimistic. I toss it in a trash can near the exit,
then head home to wait till it all turns over again,
when spring brings playoff predictions,
hope, apple blossoms, and soft rain.

Bruce W. Niedt is a southern New Jersey native, husband and father of four sons, who began the second phase of his writing life in 1999 after a long hiatus. Since then has been published in nearly a hundred online and print journals and magazines in the U.S., U.K. and Australia, including *Writer's Digest, Writer's Journal, ByLine, The Lyric, The Barefoot Muse, Lucid Rhythms, Spitball, Chantarelle's Notebook, US 1 Worksheets, Edison Literary Review, Journal of New Jersey Poets, Schuylkill Valley Journal, Tilt-a-Whirl, The Wolf,* and *paper wasp*. His work has also appeared in anthologies such as *Best of the Barefoot Muse* and *Poem You Heart Out*. He has workshopped with poets such as Billy Collins, Jane Hirshfield, Marge Piercy, Molly Peacock, and Stephen Dunn. Among his awards and honors are two Pushcart Prize nominations, two nominations for the Sundress Best of the Net Award, the ByLine Short Fiction and Poetry Prize, two first prizes for poetry at the Philadelphia Writers Conference, and five prizes of publication from *Writer's Digest* in the "Poetic Asides" poetry contests. He has recently retired after 39 years of government service, and plans to spend more of his time with poetry and his family, including his young granddaughter.

www.ingramcontent.com/pod-product-compliance
Lightning Source LLC
Chambersburg PA
CBHW060226050426
42446CB00013B/3190